for my promising skies

naked

flowers exposed

Conceived by Walter Hubert

HarperCollins*Publishers*

Flower Power

Peggy Sirota

Leonardo De Conciliis, Born December 8, 1996, Miami, Florida

Linda Churilla

Vincent, 1995

Rose and Dress

Paolo Roversi

What I love about film is the many ways it allows you to seduce the viewer into your world.

In still photography it is the challenge of telling your story in one simple image.

Marcus Burnett

Eau de Napoli

Nathaniel Goldberg

Malcolm McDowell, *Helianthus annuus,* Tuscany, 1994

George Holz

Hyacinth: a youth loved and accidentally killed by Apollo, who memorialized

him with a hyacinth growing from the youth's blood.

Duane Michals

Paul Ate the Flower

Carter Smith

Scent is the most remarkable part of a flower's beauty. The scent alone transports me into a world all its

own. Certain scents can take me back in time to when I first experienced a smell, or remind me of a

time forgotten. The smell of a flower takes me back to my youth, when I lived in the country and had all the

time in the world, playing in the fields and swimming in the pond with my brother. The smells of wild

grass and flowers were heavy in the air during the hot summer days. The heat of the sun scorched the

flowers and perfumed the air. I will never forget those timeless days when I would come upon a group

of flowers and stop so I could smell their beauty. Now that I am older and almost ready to face the world

I look back on my youth and wonder if I will ever be able to smell the world in the same way again.

Noe DeWitt

The back of a yellow ranunculus.

Toby McFarlan Pond

And she feels it almost like seduction

when her hardened hand, in which

Fevers once burned Full of nonsense,

From Far off, as if with blossoming touch,

comes to caress her hard-set chin.

—Rainer Maria Rilke, 1907

Eric Freeman

When my assistant, Keith, got married in September, they provided these little handmade packets

of sunflower seeds to throw at the bride and groom as they left the party. I kept a package

and when the spring came, I planted them in the window box of my apartment in New York City.

I did this so I could photograph the flowers for them as an anniversary present. These are the

photos, and I'm happy to say that over the year I've watched their love for each other blossom,

just as those tiny little seeds grew into these big, bright, beautiful flowers.

Stewart Shining

Two Parted Flowers

Sakeba chiru
mi no yukusue ya
hana sekai

That which blossoms
falls, the way of all flesh
in this world of flowers.

—Kiko, haiku poet

Daniel Belknap

Garden roses floating in a pool
of water.

Hypodermic needles for sale
on the street.

About 6 minutes apart.

—Marrakech, Morocco, 1996

Richard Phibbs

Springtime whisperings of her oblation

In secret creature-conversations . . .

—And lo! a listener is creeping upward

toward acceptance . . .

Susan Copen Oken

Flower, skin, and her blue dress.

Sean Dungan

I remember once when I was a kid (maybe seven or eight years old), I sent away for dozens of white hyacinth bulbs from a color catalog my mom had. I planted the bulbs in clay pots and kept them away from the light, because somewhere I had read that they should be kept in the dark until they were ready to bloom. Supposedly, they would grow longer stems, when the flowers blossomed they would not only be beautiful and scented, but they would have great long stems.

Every day they grew taller, but there were no green stems or leaves, only white stems and leaves. They finally grew so tall that they started to fall over. I thought that even though I knew nothing about growing hyacinths, my love for them was so strong it would certainly make them grow. But it didn't. I took them outside to throw away because they were never going to become what I had seen in the magazine or in my dreams.

The next day I was taking out the trash when I noticed the white stems and leaves of the hyacinths had begun to turn green. Somehow the light was changing them. They became greener, stronger, and they grew upward, becoming more beautiful. I had set them free.

Watching my hyacinths thrive, I learned about light, I learned that flowers talk: I learned to listen.

Walter Hubert

Jack-in-the-Pulpit, *Arisaema triphyllum*

There was a monk in Kyoto with a garden of rare irises that were just coming into bloom.
The Emperor of Japan heard of this exquisite garden and decided to pay him a visit.
The monk prepared tea for the ceremony on the day of the visit, but when the Emperor arrived
he found the garden cut to the ground. Upon entering the temple he saw in the place of
honor, for him to admire and enjoy, a single iris of superb perfection in a vase.

I thought of this story as I kneeled over the supreme jack-in-the-pulpit in my garden.

The jack blooms in early spring and flower over a period of two weeks. It is an endangered species
and against the law to cut. The seeds of the jack look like small cornstalks. As it dries the
flower wraps around the magenta berries. They fall in this clump into the moist earth to be covered
by fall leaves and snow. They bake for years underground, where the berries develop and
grow before they birth a small plant with three leaves that is perhaps four to five inches in height.
After a few years the first flower appears. From then on, year after year in exactly the same
spot the flowering plant reappears. Each year it grows taller and with a thicker stalk and larger leaves
than the year before. Each has a unique color and personality—some black and off-white with
purple-black pistil, others green and white with green pistil.

I've transplanted a small garden filled with them and have photographed them for over fifteen
years without ever cutting one. This was to be the first time. My husband, passing by, reminded me
that it was something I shouldn't do. Instead, I brought the vase, background paper, and
bamboo sticks out to the flower. I photographed throughout the day, lining up the vase as closely
as I could under the flower without hurting the plant.

I talk to my jacks. I sit among them. I care for them. I see them as sacred. I have
rescued broken ones floating down the creek or smashed by horses' hooves.
I love them. I've never cut one. I never will.

Sheila Metzner

Untitled

Raymond Meier

As soon as you try to

imagine improvement you collapse in recognition that

even slight imperfections

belong so completely that to question them becomes well

beyond one's length.

Maria Robledo

My interest in photographing flowers goes beyond the obvious beauty. It's an in-your-face approach and forces the viewer to see a little differently. I strip the plant bare, expose that which is often unseen, and reveal the very essence of where the beauty lies.

Tom Baril

Amaryllis, 1996

Often a painting or drawing of a single flower will intrigue me more than a photograph. I find the former more illustrative and personal. So when asked to photograph this amaryllis, I instinctively wanted to generate a more expressive image than my camera and light would typically permit.

Edward Maxey

an inexhaustible source

of divine inspiration

childlike innocence

draped without pretense

unable to pose

yet unable to provide

anything but unashamed beauty

Peter Bosch

Daffodils

Kelly Klein

Elephant Ears for Raemann

Manuel Miranda

"What is the matter?

 You don't seem to be happy."

"Oh yes, I am happy,

 but I am sad."

Ross Bleckner

Un fiore bianco, di amore irresistibile

—Pablo Neruda

Mimmo Jodice

Flowering Kale

Bill Steele

Tiger Grass: Living Skin

A living skin of young grass. The yellow and green stripes have been imprinted in the

blades of grass through the natural process of photosynthesis. The intensity of light

the blades receive corresponds precisely to the amount of chlorophyll the grass produces:

the more light the darker the green, the less light the brighter the yellow.

Heather Ackroyd and Daniel Harvey

From "The Little Pink" series

Alison Duke

Sex is a matter of interpretation. What you see might not be. What you feel will certainly be. What your heart touches

will harmonize with the deepest of your sexual being. A flower—as simple as it might be—makes me feel sexy.

Michel Haddi

One night on the outskirts of Kigali, Rwanda

She came from the large tree

And said to me,

"Sparks of life blind mankind.

Only when darkness comes does mankind open its eyes to listen,

But just the darkness remains."

The next morning I was carried to a bed in a hospital for six months

To digest what she said.

I am still blind.

Toshi Kazama

beauty

flesh

steel

Hans Gissinger

January 23, 1997

Todd Eberle

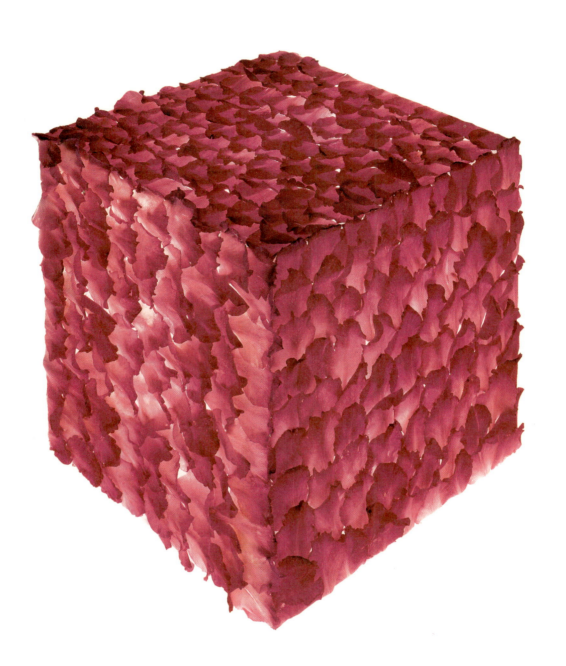

Light, crystal, vapor, drama, perfection, soaring, energy, spirit, youth, timelessness, sensuality, blossom, and light all encompassed in the splendor of a woman propelled by the flower.

Joe McBride and John Lund

The perfume of two hundred dozen roses, the beauty of the light, a perfect moment in time.

Robin Muller

Magnolias, Morton Street, 1997

Jack Pierson

I arrived at the church.

The night came in.

Then I started projecting.

Bart Kresa

Notre Dame des glans

Notre Dame des fleurs

—Jean Genet

Gilles Bensimon

Graceland, 1996

Sofia Coppola

4:00 a.m. Christmas Day. A distant, echoing thud. The roadkill dies in my backyard. He deserves better.

I want to bury him, but the ground is frozen. I want live flowers, but they freeze too easily. Plastic are

far too ugly, but I have nothing else on Christmas Day. Humans use them to remember their own dead,

so why not for a deer? Maybe they'll help keep the turkey buzzards away. I am wrong.

Peter Wert

Mingus and Baby's Breath

Danielle Weil

Growing up in the suburbs of Cleveland, Ohio, I remember (I must have been seven or eight)

wandering alone in a wooded area near our house. I felt so small beneath the big trees and yet oddly

safe and strangely excited by nature. But my favorite thing about these walks was finding a

precious patch of lily of the valley. So perfect in design, so fragile, yet so sturdy and with a fragrance

that made the larger flowers weep with envy. The years passed, and recently I had a dream that

I was that boy again, walking in those woods again, but now the trees were giant lilies of the valley.

A look back that fills me with sweet sadness.

Joel Grey

This is Stephen Kelemen's and my home in Orient Point, New York, August 1996. The boy is our godson, Bennett Williams. If you look closely, you may see the good witch Glinda in the bubble.

Lloyd Ziff

Hope can be born anywhere.

Fabrizio Ferri

Cassiope mertensia colonizes spectacular sites in the alpine zone near the timberline. It clings to or surrounds rocks for warmth. This particular niche was more unusual geologically than most. Molten granites met older metamorphic rocks, depositing heavy metals, uplifting, warping, and folding along the contact. Astonishing colors and shapes arose and were later polished by glaciation. Cracks trapped wind- and waterborne soil, cassiope rooted, and its own decay improved the site. This is the background for the cassiope rock garden, only one of the innumerable and exquisite details that expand the scale of our own existence.

Howard Weamer

Mountain Light

Spring wildflowers in Mitchell Canyon on Mount Diablo, California.

Galen Rowell

Kansas

It is recovered!
What? Eternity.
It is the sea
Mixed with the sun.

—Arthur Rimbaud

Lance Accord

Tulips Pointing at the Past

David Sims

Estella Warren, New York

Anders Overgaard

Sueños de Girasoles (Dreams of Sunflowers)

When I was a little boy in Cuba my mother always had sunflowers around the house. I remember having a very high fever and dreaming of beautiful large sunflowers floating on water with naked boys swimming underneath them and I was not able to touch them. From that day on I've always fantasized about boys and sunflowers.

Sunflowers not only light up a room, they light up the soul. I dedicate these images to all the friends I've lost and hope that when they see these photos their souls will light up. We miss you Gus, Michael, Giulio, Claudio, and Carlos.

Alexis Rodriguez-Duarte

Floral Nudes

From the seedling to the sprouting, the blossoming to the decomposing, and finally the death. This is the beauty of life. My symbols for the beauty of nature and for life are the flower and the woman.

Mark Gerhardt Squires

A dive from the darkness

A grip of the fire

A blow on your coal

To fan your desire

I feel your life

Hanging from my teeth

The steel turns red

As you tremble beneath

The gate swings open

An illusion we believe

The spread of your flesh

Will let us breathe.

Chris Nofziger

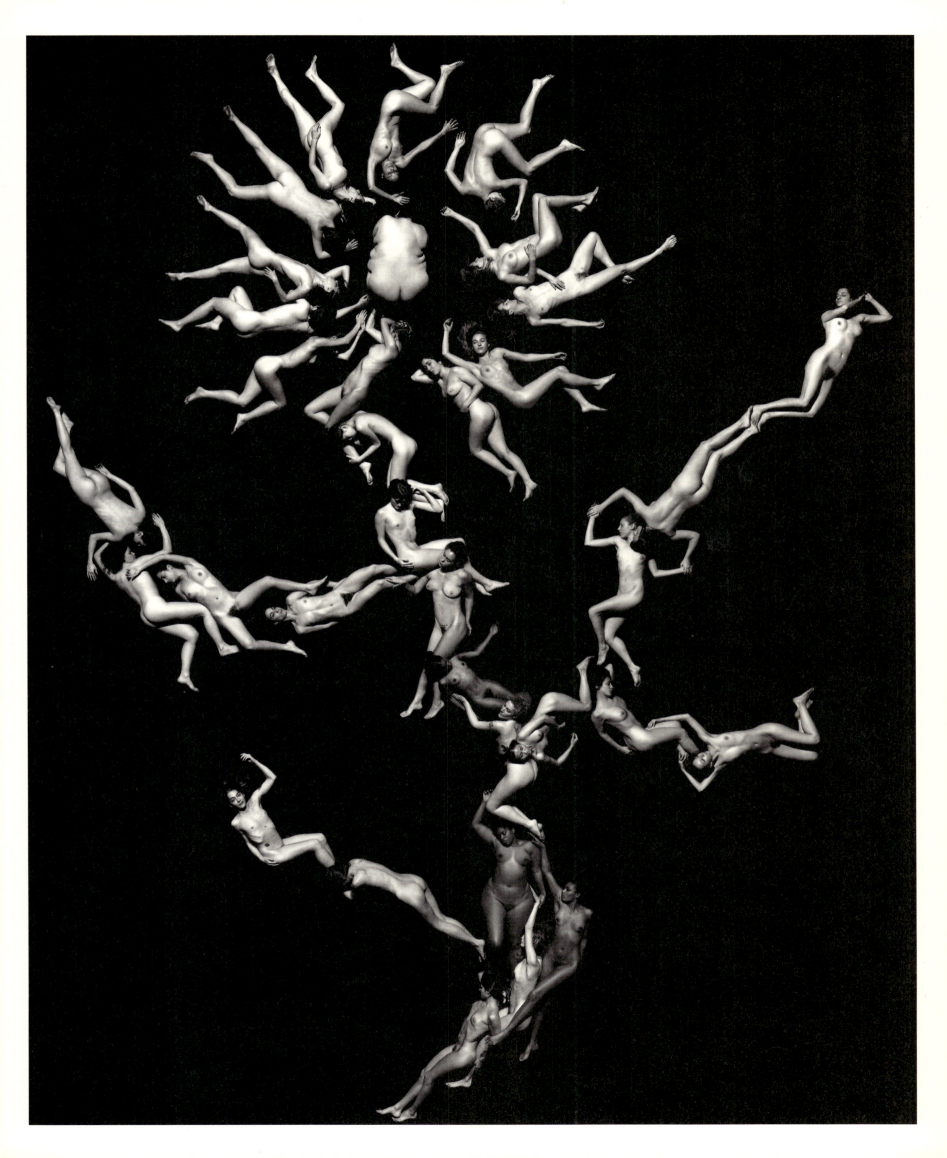

Tattoo, Rose Bowl Parade, 1997

Henry Horenstein

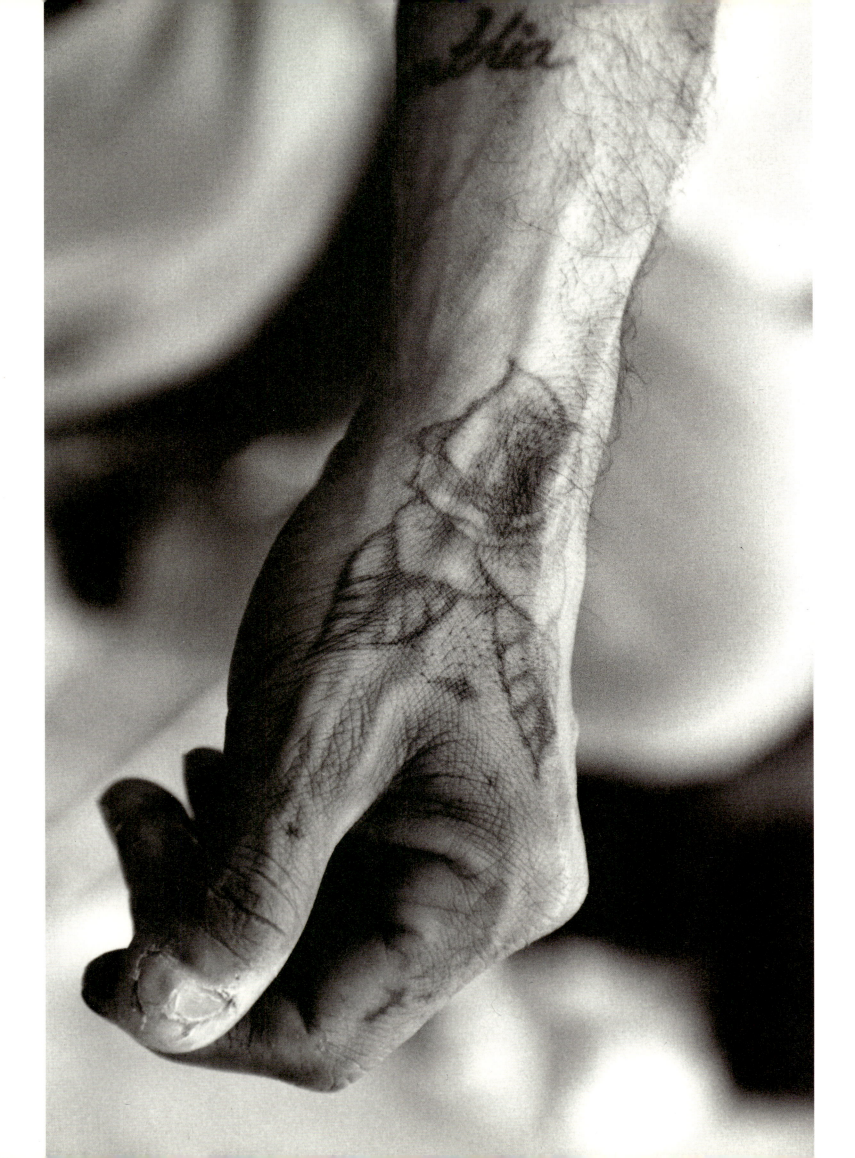

Audrey, New York, 1997

Tom Munro

Janet Planet

Brigitte Lacombe

Vous êtes un homme heureux, le nôtre . . .

—Louis XIV

Didier Malige

The true mystery of the world is the visible, not the invisible.

—Oscar Wilde

Walter Chin

Carrie in Los Angeles, November 1996

Don't fence me in.

—Cole Porter

John Patrick Salisbury

Eli for Raemann

Patricia Miranda

Claire Danes, December 1996

Firooz Zahedi

Alfin vid'io per entro I fiori e l'erba

Pensosa ir si leggiadra donna

Et avea indosso si candida gonna

Si texta ch'oro et neve

Parea insieme.

At the end I saw her among the flowers and the greenery.

She moved slowly, absorbed in her thoughts, this lovely creature.

She was wearing a skirt white as snow and her hair was blonde

So that she appeared before me like gold and snow.

—Francesco Petrarca

Manuela Pavesi

The idea was a series of pictures and a short film loosely based on the Greek goddess Daphne. To make it happen I called in favors with all of my hair, makeup, and styling friends to help shoot it.

Walter Hubert arrived early to drop off the flowers. He had to go to the airport so we went over how all of the various blossoms could be used before he left.

The crew, my dog Mud, and I piled into the van. We had driven north for about an hour when I started thinking about how I should use the flowers. As I thought about it more and more, terror jolted me, like waking up late. I didn't remember loading or seeing the flowers loaded into the van. I'd left them behind.

It was already noon and there was no way to return to the city and make it back in time to do hair, makeup, and shoot before dark. We started brainstorming and decided to check the local flower shops in Peekskill for what we needed. I hated to be negative but this was my hometown, and the only flower store I remembered was the one where I bought my prom date a powder blue corsage to match her dress. We started driving and stumbled upon a little florist. We stepped inside and the first thing we saw were pepper berries—one of the four items that we needed. If worse came to worst I could always cover her in pepper berries. Upon looking further we found another piece of the missing foliage. Some yellow stuff I don't know the name of. Two out of four. The light was already starting to fade and there were no hydrangeas. We hurried to another store to find they only had dried ones. This was no time to be picky, so we took them. Three out of four. Good enough.

We did hair and makeup and raced to the top of a hill where there was the most light. I started to shoot and a pickup truck pulled up with two understudies from the movie *Deliverance* and a wood chipper attached to the back. They parked and stared. I tried to shoot, yet all I could think about was *Fargo*. They left. I shot again. It was the last of the light and it was beautiful. Not enough speed for the movie, but at least we got the picture.

Daphne by the Tree, Radio Terrace, Peekskill, New York, 1996

John Huba

Tatjana, January 20, 1992

Herb Ritts

Untitled

Matthew Rolston

Ten years ago by the sea in northern California were a Greene and Greene house, a flower, a vase, and a sculpture.

François Halard

Three moments in the life of the rose that marks a piece of land on 11 Bank Street.

Oberto Gili

Picnic Table, End of the Day, Bellport, Long Island, Summer 1995

Pamela Hanson

"I mostly take pictures of things I love. Like girls," said Frank, pointing the lens at a vase of weeping flowers.

"Well, what the hell am I?"

"A girl, you're a girl," he responded with a snap of the shutter. "But flowers are like girls. Right, Tommy?"

"Yeah," said Tommy, slouched into a broken wicker chair. "They're cool to look at."

"Cool to look at, maybe," she snapped. "But you can't get any physical pleasure from them."

"That's why you're here."

—*Superparadise*

Michael Scalisi

My great-aunt Nell (we called her "Big" Nell after my sister "Baby" Nell was born) always loved Saint Therese. She had one

of those glass-domed snowies that enshrined a miniature statue of "the little flower." Legend had it that when

Saint Therese died the heavens opened up and rained delicate pink roses—so did "Big" Nell's snowie every time I shook it up.

This girl/saint, a Carmelite nun, is set up in my country atelier. The pink roses behind her are everlasting—plastic!

Mary Randolph Carter

Sofia in my apartment late one afternoon in November 1996, Los Angeles.

Paul Jasmin

Young Monk, Drepung Monastery, Lhasa, Tibet

Richard Gere

Coot, Treasure Beach, Jamaica, West Indies, January 1997

Berry Berensen

The Thin White Duke Preparing for Last Tour Day, Paris, 1976

The next best thing to photographing flowers is cultivating them.

Winter's end is near and I am impatient.

—1997

Andrew Kent

When I perform in theater I especially enjoy the perfume and elegance of the stargazer in my
dressing room. And the little fellow in the corner does also. Happy is one of the original Walt Disney
seven dwarfs, and has been a part of my life since I appeared in my very first movie in 1938.

Roddy McDowall

A Saint for Soccer, Naples, Italy

No more unusual than the usual.

Barbara DeWitt

Flowers, Hong Kong, 1995

Saul Fletcher

Flowers honor our loves, our triumphs, and our sorrows. In pursuit of flowers,
we come close to the face of nature. For those who watch, flowers mark the passing
of time and the seasons. Flowers die . . . and live with us.

For those who watch:
But a mere blur in the fast-spinning world about us, insignificant to the recorders
of power, time, and history, the smallest of flowers—grace notes in our refuge
from the world outside—possess the awesome power to refresh us, give us pause,
invade our lives with such tender beauty and such moment that they
alter our little world, if but for an instant, in the most significant of ways.

Tom Pritchard

For Nan

Louise Serpa

In the early sixties the legendary fashion model Dorian Leigh introduced me to a small auction house outside

of Paris near Versailles. Every Saturday there was an auction with the most wonderful antiques. Since

I was furnishing a town house in New York, I was eager to find authentic French furniture. We arrived late on

that rainy morning and the bidding was already under way. Suddenly two small flower paintings came up

for sale that caught my eye, but since we were so far back I was unsure and I lost the items during the bidding.

I always regretted not staying in there and am most grateful for this assignment to make a

photograph in the spirit of my lost treasures.

—February 10, 1997

Bert Stern

Dear Mom,

Here are the flowers I meant to pick for you when I was a child.

Love,

Your son

Jeff Olson

I can remember Mother's distant voice calling me for an early tea. Peering through the wooden fences,

climbing over the Dorset flint walls to see the colorful gardens tended by the old ladies.

In all the county there were no flower beds so lovely as theirs. Snapdragons grew there, lupines and sweet

williams, shepherd's purses and forget-me-nots bloomed and blossomed through the summer.

The swallows stretched and the church bells rang as the raspberry jam Miss Ryan had made was placed on

the table. It's a comforting thought, but whatever happens in the world there will always be a corner

of the countryside that remains forever my England.

Tim Walker

Grandmother's garden
Flowers everywhere
Wild—so bright
In their changing colours
Golden perfume in the air.

Grandmother's garden
Timeless space
Moving—lights
In their short existence
From eternity into this place.

—New York City, February 1997

Claus Wickrath

Boy in Trailer, Milan

Steven Klein

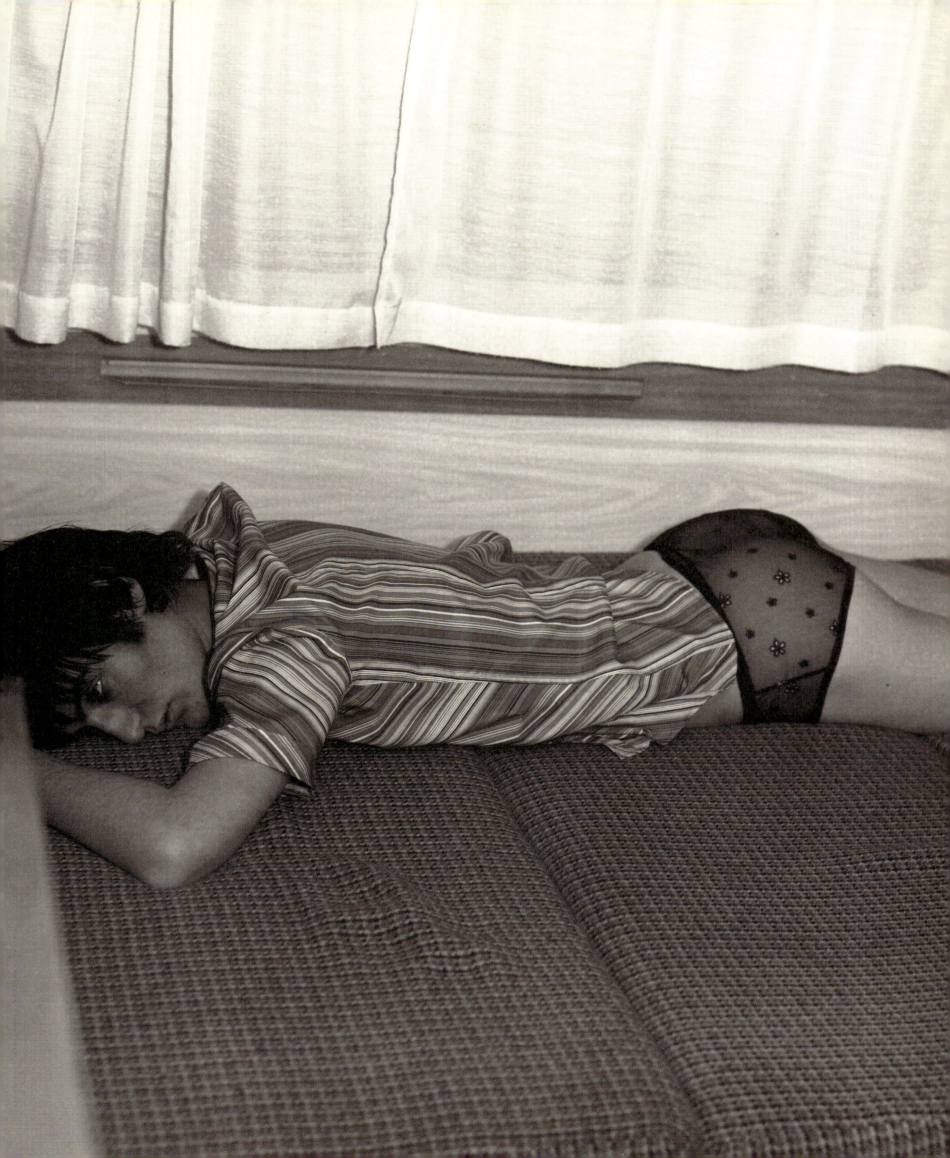

Flowered Couch with Sweet Scent

Steven Sebring

Look Both Ways

When you were four you told me, "Bugs Bunny is a good actor." You were right.

Flowers, models, and poets can only wish to have that special beauty of yours, son. You've got such an abundance; hell, you just give it away.

You are the eternally disappointed optimist, seeing all the beauty on this great earth, and at the same time feeling all of its sorrow.

It's tough being your father, knowing you have more courage and goodness than I could ever hope to muster, though I'll try before crossing the street. Look both ways, you are my beautiful little boy.

Robert Maxwell

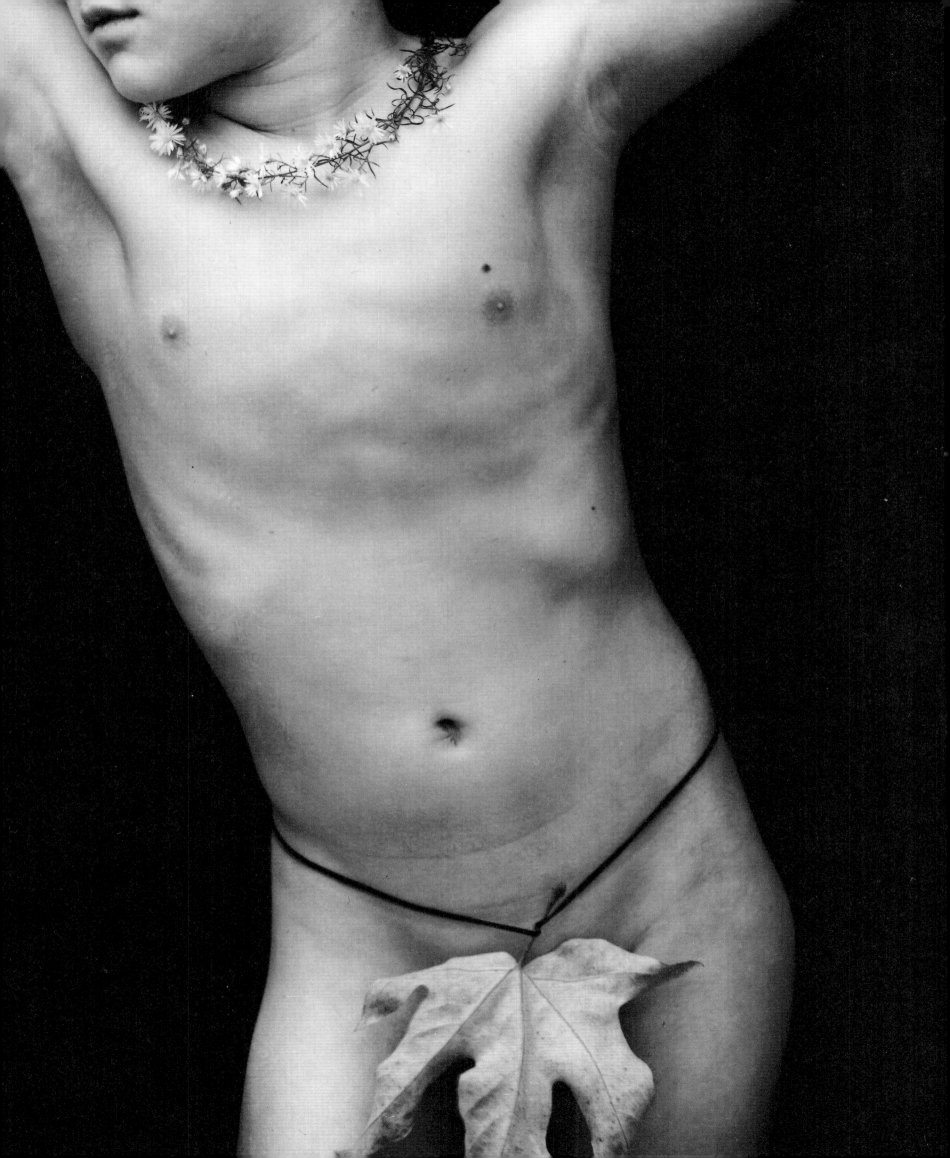

I give back to a man the pride of his vanity
To a woman, the pride of her mystery.

I always observe a thing or a form as I would watch a flower, with the
same sense of freedom that we experience when we are strolling
alone or chatting to a friend; the color of a flower or its form captures
our senses, it is mesmerizing, and we have to steal it from nature
to stay with us for the rest of our walk. We are picking it up to carry its
scent for a little time. This, to my mind, is a jewel.

—Luigi Scialanga

Androge(no)

—Alessandro Rossellini

Alessandro Rossellini and Luigi Scialanga

Linda, 1991

Steven Meisel

I've always envied photographers who could create pictures. They have a vision and they orchestrate the subject, the surroundings, and the light. And somehow—through talent and persistence—they get it right, on film. Me, I'm always looking for the accident, the thing that comes from a place I can't know or control. The more I see my hand in the frame, the less I like the photograph. I desperately want to believe that the person or thing I am photographing just magically appeared, complete in every way.

This is a scary way to work, but I'm stuck with it. And what's strange is that often enough that magic does strike, and I'm pulled along by it, and encouraged to try my luck one more time. Now!

Kurt Markus

Before that night gardenias would remind me of my mother holding me to her neck and the smell of her sweet perfume.

Shane Hallinan

Ballad for Skye

Like a soul song
I can't forget how lucky I am
that all the dogs in my life
never ate flowers
no
not like Doris Day's dog
in *Please Don't Eat the Daisies*.

Like a jazz song I can't forget
all my friends
and lovers
who gave me flowers
still, I save them all
in a book.

Like a blues song
I can't forget
my mom and
dad
growing English garden roses
way back home near wheat fields.
But was it my imagination
playing with me
that made them so pink?

Like an aria from an opera
I can't forget
when my friend
Donald died,
he wanted to be remembered
by the indulgence of delphiniums.

Like a rock 'n' roll song
I can't forget
how my new dog Skye
never eats the flowers
but he eats everything else.

Bruce Weber

Flowers frighten me. They're so beautiful, and then they die. Beauty is a disappearing act. You have to capture it before it's gone. That is why I own a camera.

But there is another kind of beauty. That of the soul, which is eternal.
Thomas, the guy in this picture, has both.

If I had a son, I would want him to be like Thomas. But no one is like Thomas.
He's one of a kind. A rare, exotic flower. He must have bloomed on Mars.

Joe Lalli

Eva in Field of Sunflowers

Ellen Von Unwerth

I bought the first lei as a joke—just a little present to celebrate being on vacation together.
A local farmer had set up his mailbox as a tiny store. You took what you wanted
from a few pieces of fruit or handstrung leis and paid by slipping some money through
a slot in the top of the box. Soon I was stopping there every time I headed home.

Our mornings became routine: a long swim in the bay, breakfast, and the very
basics of housework. The minute Stephanie stepped out of the ocean, she would wear
the fresh lei. It made her hair smell good, she said.

This was the best time to hang out. We took our cues from the height of the sun. There
was nowhere to go until the shadows were off the beach. We would make the bed together.
Stephanie always put the lei between the sheets and the pillows on top of the covers.

Dewey Nicks

Lucy '97

Dick Nystrom

Australian Wildflower, Sydney, January 1987

FOCUS is completely a property of photography. The human eye does
not see in the same way. The optical lens gives the photographer
a definite choice where the focus should or should not land. This does
not work the same way in any of the other fine arts.

OUT OF FOCUS is what I am exploring.

I am searching for the point of out of focus where a new image
becomes quite clear. The series started with a sharp flower
in the foreground with a nude body in the background out of focus,
mimicking or playing against the shape of the flower.

I continued in this direction with women, men, and couples, all
combinations of form having something different to say.

Mark Arbeit

Fresh flowers always give me a lift.

Greg Gorman

Twins are frequently born with similar thoughts, redundant in their features and regarding themselves as each other's universe. Rose petals fall from their stem in symbiotic anarchy, just as twins grow from infants to adults . . . destiny would have it no other way.

Len Prince

Cradle Song

Dream, dream, my sweet life,
of heaven, which brings the flowers;
blossoms glisten there; they quiver
to the song your mother sings.

Dream, dream, bud of my care,
of the day when the flowers sprouted,
of the bright blossoming morning
when your little soul came into the world.

Dream, dream, bloom of my love,
of the silent holy night
when the flowering of his love
made this world a heaven for me.

—Richard Strauss

John Dugdale

Petals unfold to reveal the soul of a flower, and in doing so, change its face seemingly by the moment.

A large part of my childhood was spent developing and nurturing a kinship with flowers. My love for them was heightened by stories depicting fantastic abstractions involving flowers. The area where I grew up—and still live—is called Altadena (the high view) and was famous for its vast highland slopes of golden poppies. Ship captains described them as "tongues of fire" and would focus their spyglasses on them in order to navigate the sea. My imagination was further stirred as I read stories of lovers in exotic Turkey who returned to their bridal chamber to find their bed floating in a sea of pink rose petals three feet deep.

As my career in floral design grew, I began to provide flowers and floral styling for photo shoots. As a result, I developed a rapport with many photographers and began to create a new artistic arena for myself. Just as a photographer might alter light or a camera angle to achieve a certain drama or mood, I could use shape, size, color, and texture to create a variety of feelings and attitudes within a photograph.

A few years ago, while working on a photo shoot with Bruce Weber, the subject of flowers in photography came up. We agreed that flowers seemed to play a major role in shaping the visions of many artists. We evolved the idea of bringing together the work of a group of photographers into a single volume that would pay homage to flowers. The response to my invitation was overwhelming. Each photographer was invited to contribute a photograph that would reveal his or her feelings, and in many cases, fantasies about the myriad personae of flowers. The accompanying text would elaborate on the artist's point of view. The resulting images illuminate the pages of this book with intrigue and charm.

Flowers play a greater role in our lives now more than any other time in history. They enhance our lives with their beauty, as their grace adorns our celebrations, our memorials, our passions, our loves, our truest and perhaps most inexpressible feelings. The reason for choosing a flower sometimes seems inexplicable. We may not constantly be aware of the form, scent, color, or even presence of floral influence, but the camera isolates these moments. No longer bound to the life span of a flower, I have attempted to bring the subconscious effect of flowers into conscious awareness.

Flowers hold a life within of their own, each with individual needs and personalities. It has been my privilege to act as an agent, speaking on their behalf.

Walter Hubert

Walter Hubert's expertise extends over a wide range of artistic endeavors. His formal training culminated

in a master's degree in painting and drawing from The Otis Art Institute in Los Angeles. He went

on to teach painting in England and the United States and is currently a nationally sought after lecturer on

the art of floristry and event design. Walter has been a design consultant for advertising layouts; his

clients include designers Ralph Lauren, Gianni Versace, and Calvin Klein and photographer Bruce Weber.

He was chosen to judge the Pasadena Tournament of Roses Parade and subsequently created many

award-winning floats. His company, Silver Birches, is known for its high-quality and stylish presentations

in custom floristry for individuals and corporate clients. Through Silver Birches, Walter has been

a creative source of innovative and exciting designs nationwide.

Credits and Acknowledgments

Marcus Burnett Model: Mike Hendricks
Print: Chelsea Black and White

Walter Chin Model: Adam Kavanagh
Stylist: Paul Sinclair

Linda Churilla Model: Henrietta Southam de Concilis
Stylist: Anuschka
Assistant: Chris Fanning

Barbara DeWitt To Donald, who taught me how to see.

Noe DeWitt Model: Dylan Esworthy

John Dugdale Model: Dirk J. Platzek

Greg Gorman Model: Omry Reznik
Hair: Livio
Makeup: Lisa Ruckh-Dodd
Props: Ron Oats set design
Fine art iris watercolor prints by ZZYZX Visual Systems
Special thanks to Joel West.

Shane Hallinan Models: Samantha Story and Tami Wong

John Huba Model: Junco Smith
Stylist: Karen Eisenberg
Makeup: Lorraine Leckie
Hair: Ashley Xavier

Paul Jasmin Model: Sofia Coppola
Makeup: Jo Streddle

Andrew Kent Barbara DeWitt

Joe Lalli Model: Thomas Naporano
Agency: Click
Hair: Eric Gabriel
Print: Chelsea Black and White

Steven Klein Model: Matthew

Didier Malige Model: Janine
Hat: Patricia Underwood
Hair: Salvador Calvano
Makeup: Fulvia Farolfi

Kurt Markus Model: Corey Corbin
Hair: Edris Nichols and Kazue Kuwabara, Tricomi Hair Salon

Joe McBride and John Lund Model: Sarah Elwell
Stylist: Alayne Patrick

Steven Meisel Model: Linda Evangelista
Hair: Garren
Makeup: Kevyn Aucoin
Fashion Editor: Paul Cavaco
Flowers: Denise Oppizzi

Duane Michals Flower: Hydrangea
Model: John Painter

Chris Nofziger Minerva Durham/Spring Studio
Rob White/Pier 59 Studio
Prudence Whittlesey
Ann Giordano
Richard Reed
Wendell R. Maruyama
Catering: Pamela D'Orazio

Anders Overgaard Model: Estella Warren
Hair: Frederick Parnell
Makeup: Sandrine van Slee

Manuela Pavesi Model: Rachel Kirby

Len Prince Models: Ian Hundley and Mark Hundley

Herb Ritts Hair: Serena Radaelli
Makeup: George Newell
Stylist: Sarajane Hoare

Alexis Rodriguez-Duarte Models: Bruno Lavoie and Gary Taylor
Grooming: Tico Torres
Assistants: Nick Garcia and Charles Rodriguez
Location: Lisa Lawrence, Golden Beach
Labs: Eric @ BWC Lab, Sixty-eight Degrees Lab, LTI, Lab
Equipment: Howard at Aperture Professional Supply

Alessandro Rossellini and Luigi Scialanga Model: Fabrizio Mele
Studio: Studio Pietro Galletti Roma
Computer Graphics: Sabina Leoni and Alessandro Rossellini
Flowers: Luigi Scialanga

John Patrick Salisbury Model: Carrie Hayes
Hair and Makeup: Julianna Sanning
Styling: Shanon Hetz
Assistants: Jennifer Salisbury and Henri Bristol

Steven Sebring Model: Angela Lindvall

Peggy Sirota Model: Antonio Banderas

Bill Steele August Bandal, Marie-Ange Bovee,
Jonathan Burroughs, Deborah Goldberg, Sheldon Goldberg,
Greenwich Orchids, Healthcheck, Beryl Lievano

Bert Stern Assistants: Richard Reed and Erskine Childers
Props: Michael Morelli
Studio: Studio 450
Other: Newel Art Galleries and Dennis Taylor Trucking

Ellen Von Unwerth Model: Eva Herzigova
Hair: Ward
Makeup: Regine Bedot
Stylist: Alice Gentilucci

Claus Wickrath Model: Georgianna Robertson
Makeup: Carmon Springs
Hair: Fred van de Bunt
Styling: Lars Nord
Assistants: Albert Torres and Orla Maguire
Studio: Pier 59 Studios
Camera Assistants: Andy Heatherington and Kevin Sweeney

Firooz Zahedi Model: Claire Danes
Hair: Chris MacMillan
Makeup: Lutz
Stylist: Linda Medvine
Floral Headpiece: Nick Tortorecci

General credits and thanks to:
Studio 59, Antonio Bellono
Tribeca Studios, Derek Lacey
Betty Eng
Carlos Frederico Farina
LTI Labs
Lexington Labs
Manny Miranda-Film
Silvain D'Houtcourt-Film Assistant
Greg Gorman Studios

Type in this book is set in Futura. Inspired by the Dutch De Stijil and Russian Constructivism movements, Futura was designed by the German book designer Paul Renner in 1927. Based on the Bauhaus school ideology "forms follows fuction", Renner used a T-square, triangle, and compass to create this geometric typeface. Futura is widely used by comtemporary designers for its crisp lines and formal simplicity. The Book is printed on Gardamatt, 135gr. paper.

HarperCollins books may be purchased for educational, business, or sales promotional use. For information please write: Special Markets Department, HarperCollins Publishers, Inc., 10 East 53rd Street, New York, NY 10022.

Printed in Italy by Amilcare Pizzi S.p.A., Milan

FIRST EDITION

ISBN 0-06-757440-8   97 98 99 00 01 / P 10 9 8 7 6 5 4 3 2 1

Designed by Sam Shahid